709.2 BLO

D0505147

Sandra Blow

Space and Matter

1958 – 2001

Due to.

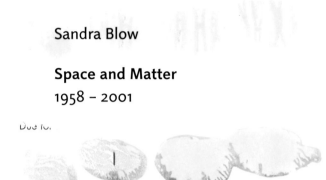

26 0065595 2

Sandra Blow in her studio, St Ives, 2001   Photograph Bob Berry

Sandra Blow

Space and Matter
1958 – 2001

Essay by Mel Gooding

St IVES

TATE

PUBLISHED TO ACCOMPANY
THE EXHIBITION AT TATE ST IVES
15 DECEMBER 2001 – 10 MARCH 2002

ISBN O 9539924 3 8

A catalogue record for this publication
is available from the British Library

© Tate Trustees 2001
All rights reserved

EDITED BY
Susan Daniel-McElroy, Andrew Dalton
and Kerry Rice

DESIGN   Groundwork, Skipton
PHOTOGRAPHY   Bob Berry
REPRODUCTION   Scantec Group, Falmouth
PRINT   Rowe the Printer, Cornwall

Contents

Introduction

Space and Matter

SUSAN DANIEL-MCELROY

facing page
Sandra Blow (b 1925)
Cornwall 1958
Oil, plaster and sacking on wood
1117 × 940mm
© the artist

Something happens to your reflective capacity when you find yourself in another country. It is as if dislocation from the day-to-day allows the mind to clear when it would otherwise be submerged. Sitting in the Zen dry garden of the Nanzenji Temple, Kyoto, Japan recently, I was transfixed by the tranquillity of this famous sixteenth-century garden.

I stared at length at the dark forms that irregularly emerged from the fine combings of the grey gravel which surrounded them. After twenty minutes, it occurred to me that what was singular about these rocks was their asymmetry, and that it was the denial of formal symmetry in their placement which had intrigued and fascinated visitors for over 500 years. I wondered if it was the searching for this idea that created the conditions for tranquillity for those seeking a Zen experience.

In the next thought my mind flew to the work of Sandra Blow whose show we had been preparing. In thinking about Blow's painting it is inevitable that ideas about colour, texture and form predominate, but until experiencing the Zen dry garden of Nanzenji Temple, I had overlooked the continuing sense of asymmetry that her paintings express. Sandra later confirmed that the denial of symmetry has been a predominant focus throughout her career. This is a huge ambition in a world that often demands the graceful coherence of beauty, and is a remarkable achievement.

I first encountered Blow's paintings in an exhibition at the Royal Academy and the Hayward Gallery in the late 1970s. As a student of painting I was in awe of the confidence of her ability – the colour and texture in her work and the use of charcoal on blank areas of canvas, held such vigour and excitement for me. I wanted to paint like her.

As Curator of Tate St Ives, I am delighted to have the opportunity of realising this exhibition. Selected by myself and my colleague Andrew Dalton, our aim was to bring together key paintings spanning 50 years and represent important moments in Sandra Blow's work.

Sandra's choice of Roger Hilton, Ben Nicholson, Alberto Burri, Karel Appel and Antoni Tapies from the Tate Collection for her *Artists on Artists* display is revealing in its rigor, and I thank her for investing her time and energy into this aspect of the show.

I am particularly grateful to Mary Bustin, Tate's Painting Conservator, for her sensitive advice on the frightening prospect of loosening large paintings from their stretchers, and her part in preparing the exhibition.

Mel Gooding, author, lecturer and critic has contributed an outstanding essay to the catalogue that brings new thoughts to bear on the artist's work and we are deeply appreciative.

Our grateful thanks are also due to the Tate St Ives Members for their vital financial contribution enabling conservation on key works.

Finally, we are deeply indebted to the artist for her ongoing commitment and enthusiasm to this project and for making new work for our exhibition, despite the ongoing delays caused by building works at her studio.

'An Artist of Nature'

MEL GOODING

Sandra Blow (b 1925)
Space and Matter 1959
Oil on board
1518 × 1226mm
© the artist

1 NATURE AND ART

Sandra Blow is an artist of nature whose work reflects a profound interest in the nature of art. The 'nature' in her paintings is never simply descriptive of things seen in the external world, for she is by no means a landscape artist, and never has been. And the aspect of 'art' that demands attention in her paintings is never a matter of specific reference to the art of others, for hers is not 'art about art', and neither does it represent a conscious and deliberate effort to extend art's possibilities, to take the next step, to assert originality. Her painting is never ironic or reflexive in mood. Its propositions are not philosophical in any self-conscious way. Her work betrays no interest in the reductive dogmas that determined the manner and look of a great deal of the boring American post-painterly abstraction that was deeply fashionable at the time when she was making her own reputation as an artist of distinctive originality. Neither has her work ever been concerned with the expression of feelings, or the conveyance of personal emotions.

What do I mean, then, by 'an artist of nature'? I mean that her painting has persistently responded to the textures and dynamics of the natural world, and found thrilling analogies for them in a variety of materials that have often themselves been taken directly into her art out of nature. Blow has a preternatural sense of the multifarious surfaces of the world and of the energies that create them, of its ceaseless motion, of its variegations of gleam, glow, shimmer and shadow, its space and light. Her paintings and collages do not attempt to picture these things as we see them, so much as to present us with a primary event that has something of the qualities of the phenomenal world we actually experience, but which adds to and intensifies that experience in a manner that is unique to a particular kind of abstract art. Blow has been committed throughout her entire career to that species of intuitive abstraction that discovers – makes visible – the hidden principles of nature, its tensions and balances, the energetic principles that counter its tendencies to disorder and chaos. Her art invents visible relations of space, colour and shape that are like the features of nature's own ever-changing face.

In saying that her work exhibits a deep concern with the nature of art I intend to identify a particular quality in the work. It is that every painting (or painting collage) by Blow is self-declarative in its disposition of materials, it never disguises the manner of its making, or the qualities of the materials of its making. From the moment of your first encounter it is obdurately, or better to say *exultantly,* what it is: an object constructed by hand and eye out of given materials. Whatever your imagination suggests (and it is in the nature of our looking at any painting that our mind makes associations: that is, in part, what the painting is there for) – here a wave, perhaps, there a tree, here darkness, there light, here an object, there space – your eye returns involuntarily, inevitably to the thing itself, finds itself responding to its colours, its textures, exploring relations of one shape to another, of one kind of material to another. And then, to a consideration (yes! the eye cannot operate without the mind, we cannot *see* without thought) of its relation as an object to the space in which you find it (a gallery with the sea and sky visible, say, or a domestic room, or the studio). In other words, you will have entered into a vital relation to it as part of your life.

Now, it is of course true that every painting is an object, and that we encounter it in a space that will affect our response, shape our definition of its meaning. When we look at a painting that pictures the visible world, whether landscape, still life, domestic interior, figures in space, at whatever scale, in whatever style, we cannot avoid thinking about the circumstances *within* the picture, of its fictional space, its fictional time, or of the objects in the picture, with all their associations. We may think about the style of the painting, its use of colour, the degrees of its departure from conventions of representation, all those things we describe as its formal qualities, but some crucial aspect of its meaning will have to do with the things depicted. The difference is that these paintings of Blow's offer the formal experience as primary: their size and shape, their design and construction, the choice of their media and materials, all have as their first purpose to create the circumstance of those vital relations between the viewer and the work as an object, and between the viewer, the object and the space around it.

There are, as well, types of abstract art that are as different from Blow's as is the figurative art just discussed. Geometric abstraction, for example, which depends upon our recognition of certain universal areas and forms, and of their regular or determined spatial relations in two or three dimensions, or on patterns of interval as between sounds, tones and colours. Blow certainly uses shapes that have a geometric look to them – rough triangles, circles, curving rhomboids etc – but these are shapes that simply occur in the work, just as they occur in nature, though never exact. Such moments in the paintings that suggest programme of colour or interval of shape are purely arbitrary, they just happen to be what they are. Then there are various kinds of transcendental abstraction, so called, whose purposes are to induce meditative states of mind or hint at the spiritual realities behind the veil of appearances. Blow's work is resolutely visible; it works not by suggestion or by mystical repetition but by being what it is to the eye.

There is also gestural or painterly abstraction, in which the paint on the canvas is a visible record of the work's creation, each stroke or colour is seen as directly, urgently expressive, and the complete work as an occasion for heightened awareness and invention on the part of the viewer. Blow's abstraction has something in common with this latter, but it lacks expressive intention in its detail, its construction is cooler and more considered, it has no designs upon the viewer: for all its astonishing bravura it is impersonal.

2 EARTH WIND AND FIRE

Blow acknowledges the personal influence on her of Alberto Burri, the great Italian artist with whom she spent a formative year in Italy in the late 1940s when she was in her early twenties. Burri was passionate about art: '[my painting] is an irreducible presence that refuses to be converted into any other form of expression,' he wrote in 1955. 'My painting is a reality which is part of myself, a reality I cannot reveal in words.' His belief in the centrality of art to life reinforced Blow's sense of vocation, and together they spent months looking at classical, gothic and renaissance architecture, at frescoes and paintings. It was not long after the war and much of the land was wasted and barren. There were no tourists and the classical ruins, the run-down palazzi and churches and the paintings they contained were time-worn and as yet unrestored. 'It was like being in paradise.' It is inconceivable that a young and gifted artist with a heightened feeling for the subtle textures and natural colour of things would not be deeply affected by such an experience. In 1949 she returned to London, aware that if she stayed she would be overwhelmed by both Burri's potent artistic personality and the inescapable pathos and beauty of Italy: 'I couldn't work in Italy in those early years. I had to get back to London... where all the experiences of my life were rooted in order to make something of what I'd learned.'

Sandra Blow produced work in the 1950s that is as vigorous and powerful as that of any abstract painting by her British contemporaries. She found her own way when she adapted Burri's use, in his own version of *art informel,* of rough and non-artistic found materials, especially sacking. Beyond this use of unconventional materials (and in this respect his influence was at this time widespread and international) too much can be made of Burri's 'influence' on her work of this period. Blow's creative preoccupations were her own, to do with effects of actions, natural and artistic, on the surface of things. The materials in her work are simply what they are; they carry no symbolic freight, they imply nothing emotional or philosophical in themselves. There is a powerful emotive poignancy to the art of Burri, a kind of rhetoric almost classical in its import, a deliberative ordering that confers upon his 'poor' materials a monumental dignity. Blow's deployment of materials is more haphazard, her handling of them rougher and readier, more provisional. She is working in fact with her own, quite different, aesthetic, one that takes the world itself as unpredictable, and finds its configurations beautiful in their waywardness. Her own 'found' materials – as well as sacking she used plaster, sand, concrete and sawdust – are themselves unmalleable and awkward in application; even her sacking, in the paintings, is irregular, it bunches, sags and snags. When she uses oil paint it gets thickened into the consistency of pitch or of mud spattered against a wall.

In both *Cornwall* (1958) and *Space and Matter* (1959) one senses the memory not so much of worn Italian frescoes, or the beauty of faded stucco, as of weathered barns, fired moorland and wind-eroded hillsides. *Cornwall,* notwithstanding its rich Italian terracotta, was painted in fact in an improvised barn studio at Lower Tregerthen, a farm on the windswept shoulder of fields above the cliffs and below the moors at Zennor, where she lived and worked for a year in 1957–58. It registers the artist's response to things seen close to, to the textured and abraded walls of farm buildings, to the discarded unravelling sacking one encounters in the farmyard, to the tarred timbers of a cowshed: this is the surface of the world as found. Blow has told how she put paintings on the top of the steps to the barn loft to see them from afar in the context of the landscape: 'The interaction with the work [of barn and landscape] was very powerful and interesting.' After her return to London in 1959 Blow would drive down to the wilder reaches of Exmoor and Dartmoor, and paint with her canvas strapped to the spare wheel on the back of her jeep. This was not to paint *from* nature, rather to paint *in* nature.

These procedures reveal that the work was conceived and made as integral to the world of objects and energies, continuous with the landscape rather than a depiction of it. In these accounts the artist is not an observer of phenomena so much as an agent of nature. *Space and Matter* has the phenomenal feel of its subject: the necessary opposition of its title is not of grand abstractions but evokes, rather, particular actualities of earth in air, open to the elements of wind and rain, its surface scorched by fire. In both this painting and *Cornwall* the artist exploits the abrasive resist of the wood or board support to the brush as a physical fact with visible effects (an aspect of art) and as an evocative analogy to the ways in which the surfaces of things in the world – plank and plaster, clay and chalk, field and furrow – are shaped and weathered by usage and erosion (an aspect of nature). In these paintings it is reference to the elements of earth, wind and fire that predominate. (Blow actually experimented at times, unsuccessfully, with the effects of burning on the support, using a blowtorch.) Her later work is no less a response to the elements, but from the late 1960s it has been lighter and brighter, more open and clear.

3 TENSION AND CLARITY

We speak of 'holding' a moment's perception, of keeping in sharp focus, for that moment, a visual complex of light, colour, space, objects and their texture, knowing that our apprehension of it cannot last. We know that our perception is always of things in a state of transition between one state and another, and this consciousness of our perceptive faculty is called *apperception*. We live in an actuality that is contingent and temporal, a state of endlessly becoming; we consciously or intuitively create a reality in which things cohere and are given meaning. What is actual exists independent of our knowledge of it in all its aspects; our reality is what we make of the stream of data the world provides us. It is the constructive imagination that creates this reality, that discovers in the flux of the world continuities, resemblances and analogies. Out of repeated moments of recognition – 'the intuitive perception of the similarity in dissimilars' – we make and re-make our reality, in continuous improvisation (making use of what comes to hand, or eye, or ear etc). We live in a condition of uncertainty alleviated by the apperceptive faculty. Sandra Blow is a poet of apperception.

In 1982 Blow made a number of collage-paintings that have in common their square format, their four-foot-by-four dimensions and their board support. These form a distinct group out of many more, similarly square, created between 1978 and 1982. (In 1978 she exhibited a group of nine four-foot-square collages, together with a number of paintings, at the second Hayward Annual; and there is a photograph of her studio in 1981 that reveals work in progress on a dozen somewhat smaller square collages.) Five of the 1982 works are represented in this exhibition, each of which combines acrylic paint with different combinations of materials such as sacking, plaster and paper; in each the acrylic has a distinct colour or tonal register. The dappled texture of the board surface is such as to give the thin acrylic covering of each painting (opaque in every case but that of *White Collage*) a delicate atmospheric shimmer, a *spatial* illusion essential to its over-all visual effect.

These works demonstrate Blow's extraordinary ability to place elements in a space in such a way as to present the illusion of a moment of poise, an instant of perfect coherence. To speak of 'placing elements in space' is to define an effect of art: the 'elements' are flat shapes; the 'space' is a plane of colour. The surface shimmer and its suggestion of atmospheric light is common to each of the paintings, but particular effects differ from one to another: the white near-triangular apertures in *Sacking, Brown and White* and *Sacking, Indigo and White*, for example, suggest a kind of aperture on to bright light behind a darker mist, with the sacking shapes configured in the gap; the white shapes balanced precariously within the inner triangle of *Red and White* appear to be solid forms against a red luminosity; the white shape *in Beige, Plaster and Red* appears to cantilever out from the right as a solid form (an effect intensified by the opaque textured plaster at centre); the opaque white paper rhombus at top left of *White Collage* appears as a blind-screen against an ambiguous space, at once a plane of raw board and white acrylic (its flatness emphasised by purely linear elements) and a spatial evocation of cloudy atmospherics.

This is merely to describe, from the vantage of one pair of eyes, the strange and contradictory conditions of space and light within which the architectonics of design in these paintings are held in tension. We are presented with flat shapes in planar space. At first we may read them, as a matter of perceptual habit, as forms or apertures in three-dimensional space, and then we imagine them as in active tension, shape against shape, in a perfect abstract clarity, a colour that is pure colour, a space that is for the eye only, an atmosphere that has none of the contingent qualities of weather. These paintings do not represent things in the recognisable spaces of the world so much as the contradictory energies that hold things in place, the 'push and pull' of things (as Blow herself puts it). Or rather, they enact analogically that moment of perception that holds things still. In this the pleasure they give is not unlike that we enjoy when we marvel at a dry stone wall or a balancing act. Each component is necessary to the maintenance of this visual poise.

The square is in itself a principle of equipoise, each side equal, each relation balanced itself to itself. No small part of the compositional tension in these collage paintings derives from the relation of the irregular poise, intuitively arrived at, of the design, and the perfect regularity, ideal and absolute, of the constraining rectangle. Each internal component strains against the square, proposes another kind of balance, asymmetric, imperfect, natural rather than geometric. The square configures into the grid that is the architectural paradigm of modernist architecture (and of much modernist art). Through the 1970s Blow had collaborated with an architect, and she thought a great deal about the work of Mies van der Rohe, the architect whose work most rigorously conformed to that paradigm. Significantly, Blow's presentation of the nine square collages at Hayward '78 was in a grid formation, effectively an orchestration of the asymmetric and irregularly internal components within the individual squares against the larger square of the con-figuration as a whole.

She spoke then about painting as indirectly influencing design in the culture as a whole, in architecture, dress, furniture, acting 'to counter the discord and disharmony of life'. She continued: 'Painting is almost biological – it is about good proportion and the balance we need for every movement.' Her latest work, created specially for this exhibition, similarly configures its components – twelve colour squares with what she has called 'off-slant' collage elements – into a grid: the architectonics of poise, of asymmetric balance, is played against the regular architecture of the individual squares and the geometry of the rectangular grid. Geometry is a mental construct; perception is a function of the biological imperative to relate to the contingent world. Blow's creative procedures, as I have suggested, are analogous to the act of perception as it is modified by conscious control. She favours collage because it enables her to make constant apperceptive adjustments: add a colour-shape here, subtract a colour-shape there, move this shape to that side, that shape to this side. And then? the moment of coherence! – 'a balance of space, colour and shape, held in a pictorial structure'; the visual poetry of 'a great clear simplicity'.

4 LIGHT, WATER AND AIR

Sandra Blow's finest early works, the oil and found-material paintings of the late 1950s and early '60s, are dominated by a consciousness of the elemental earth and its objects, broken, eroded and abraded by wind and weather. They are thickened and textured by accretions of matter, their colour-tones those of clay and chalk, or of things stained or burnt. The great works of the 1980s and early '90s, by contrast, achieve their glorious clarity and simplicity by a joyous response to the light, and to the quick evanescence of things elementally aqueous and atmospheric. They work by reduction and economy, exploiting the near translucency of thin acrylic wet washed or dry brushed on canvas. They have a spectacular boldness: they are of a scale to envelop the viewer; they are made in ways that immediately declare themselves to the eye; they feature primary and brightly chromatic local colour and great open spaces of light or dark; they are resolutely abstract but replete with visual implication. Above all, they have what Blow has called 'a startling rightness': each colour-shape 'perfect in its place, [having] an unexpected quality about it, an element of surprise.'

The two earliest works in this late manner, *Vivace* (1988) and *Glad Ocean* (1989), share the brave candour of an explosive colour splash, the once and forever throw of bright liquid acrylic in an unpredictable figure across the huge plane of the off-white primed canvas. The force of the throw translates into the image of the energy of a great spume such as we see when a powerful wave hits an obstacle, or breaks on a hidden off-shore rock: these are two of the biggest splashes in painting. To define these as 'images of energy' is to be exact to their cause and to their effect: they are not pictures of waves or splashes; they are not 'pictures' of anything. They are, precisely, what they appear to be, the traces of colour stain consequent on the action that created them. A centrifugal spatter of liquid edges these brilliant colour-gestures (for want of a better term: 'mark' and 'form' are imprecise and inadequate to their natural grandeur) to catch the effect of the moment and intensify the visual excitement of the asymmetric pictorial dynamic. To one side of each splashed figure Blow has added fragments of collage like bright splinters of colour or light, whose ambiguous direction of flight adds paradox to the images. In terms of communicative strategy these fragments add sign to trace; they are the components of the over-all image that have been selected (from among the numerous off-cuts on the studio floor) and deliberatively 'placed' alongside the 'natural' outcome of an act (albeit artistic) that could not be predicted or essentially changed. We are reminded by these, and by the arbitrary framing devices painted at the canvas edges, that this is not a work of nature, it is a work of art.

Brilliant Corner (1993) and *Selva Oscura* (1993) present us with images altogether more controlled, having something of the qualities of the mid-career collage paintings, depending upon the decisions and indecisions, the visions and revisions of the apperceptive faculty as it moves towards the composition of a moment apprehended in time and space. These are paintings which represent the darkness that by opposition defines light and colour. I like to fancy that the former is an image of urban experience: the bright shaft of vertical white light is like the street light between tall buildings (as Barnett Newman's famous 'zip' may be sometimes fairly imagined as a response to Manhattan); the irregular diagonal shaft to the left edge of the canvas is like the lateral light that comes suddenly, brightly, as you reach the corner of a block. In the latter (and the title

NOTES AND REFERENCES

Sandra Blow is quoted from a studio discussion with Sarah O'Brien Twohig published in the catalogue to her exhibition at the Royal Academy of Arts, February–March 1994; from an unpublished transcript of a conversation with Hilly Janes (September 2001); and from a conversation with the author in October 2001. Alberto Burri's statement is from *The New Decade: 22 European Painters and Sculptors*, the catalogue to an exhibition at the Museum of Modern Art, May–August 1955.

Aristotle, defining metaphor in the *Poetics*, wrote of 'the intuitive perception of the similarities in dissimilars'.

'The informing imagination', wrote Coleridge, 'reveals itself in the balance or reconciliation of opposite or discordant qualities: of sameness with difference; of the general with the concrete; the idea, with the image...', *Biographia Literaria*, 1817.

'apperception n. the mind's perception of itself as a conscious agent; an act of voluntary consciousness, merged with self-consciousness; the conscious assimilation of a new sense-experience to others already in the mind.' *Chambers Dictionary* 1998 ed.

encourages this invention) I imagine the zigzag shafts of primaries, green and white as the break-up of light through trees, as if the resinous atmosphere of the wood had acted upon it as a prism. These are indeed fanciful free associations, but they are mine, and I am entitled to them, knowing full well that what I am contemplating is a purely abstract painting, and that it therefore invites me to imagine. Any doubt I might have about its objective status will be removed as I press close to the painting and observe the vitality of detail, the undisguised artifice of brush-stroke and collage addition, the arbitrary disposition of material elements. Such satisfying local complications and complexities of texture will be found in any of these later paintings. I step back and these works configure into darkness and light, colour and texture, invite me to compose them as phenomena, like all the other things they have joined in the world.

It is difficult not to feel that *Porthmeor* (1996), the first large painting that Sandra Blow made on her return to St Ives, is not a direct and thrilling response to the light of the town and of the bay after which it is named. Not that extraordinary sunlight brightness of mid-morning to mid-afternoon, when sand and sea match each other in reflective brilliances of gold and turquoise (DH Lawrence's 'infinite Atlantic, all peacock-mingled colour'), but the early morning misty translucence of late autumn, winter or early spring, with its infinite subtleties of white and pale green, when things shimmer and loom out of the liquescent light. Even so, it is important to remember that Blow's images are made in the studio out of the materials and energies of art, thinned acrylic washes, traces of movements, that they are discovered in the intuitive processes of judgement and adjustment, the trial and error of balance and contrast that finally creates the pictorial structure – the poise and tension – that gives the work its own identity, primary and unique. The radiant architecture of colour-light that makes *Porthmeor* a beautiful event is an effect of art not an imitation of nature; it is a reality, nevertheless, that would not exist without a lifetime of attention to the changing actuality of nature, to the light of many mornings in many places.

Sandra Blow (b 1925)
Oil Drawing 1959
Oil and charcoal on paper
1194 × 1105mm
© the artist

Sandra Blow (b 1925)
Green and White 1969
Acrylic, ash, charcoal and collage on canvas
3048 × 3048mm
© the artist

Sandra Blow (b 1925)
Beige, Plaster and Red 1982
Acrylic and plaster on board
1220 × 1220mm
© the artist

Sandra Blow (b 1925)
Sacking, Indigo and White 1982
Acrylic, mixed media on board
1220 × 1220mm
© the artist

Sandra Blow (b 1925)
Sacking, Brown and White 1982
Acrylic, mixed media on board
1220 × 1220mm
© the artist

Sandra Blow (b 1925)
Red and White 1982
Acrylic on board
1220 × 1220mm
© the artist

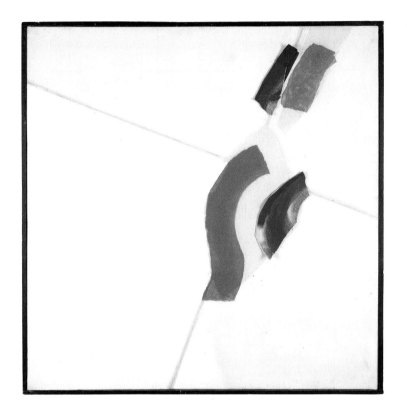

Sandra Blow (b 1925)
Red White Blue 1982
Acrylic and collage on board
1220 × 1220
© the artist

Sandra Blow (b 1925)
Mauve, Brown and White 1982
Acrylic and collage on board
1220 × 1220mm
© the artist

Sandra Blow (b 1925)
Vivace 1988
Acrylic and collage on canvas
2600 × 2600mm
© the artist

Sandra Blow (b 1925)
Glad Ocean 1989
Acrylic and collage on canvas
2600 × 3660mm
© the artist

Sandra Blow (b 1925)
Selva Oscura 1993
Acrylic and collage on canvas
2590 × 2600mm
© the artist

Sandra Blow (b 1925)
Brilliant Corner II 1993
Acrylic and collage on canvas
2200 × 3100
© the artist

Sandra Blow (b 1925)
TranquillO 1993
Acrylic, mixed media and collage on canvas
2690 × 2690mm
© the artist

Sandra Blow (b 1925)
Porthmeor 1996
Acrylic on canvas
2590 × 2600mm
© the artist

Sandra Blow (b 1925)
Zen 2001
Acrylic and canvas on canvas
1060 × 1060mm
© the artist

Sandra Blow (b 1925)
Reeling Water 2001
Acrylic, mixed media and collage on canvas
2590 × 2600mm
© the artist

Sandra Blow (b 1925)
Resounding 2001
(twelve-part work)
Acrylic on canvas
4568 × 3401 installation
(individual 1067 × 1067mm)
© the artist

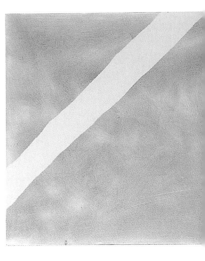

Selected Biography

Sandra Blow RA, HON. FRCA

Sandra Blow was born in London and studied at St Martin's school of Art, London, The Royal Academy Schools, London and L'Accademia di Belle Art, Rome.

1961 – 1975 Tutor, Painting School, Royal College of Art
Elected Associate of the Royal Academy
Elected Royal Academician
Appointed Honorary Fellow, Royal College of Art

WORKS INCLUDED IN THE COLLECTION OF

Tate
Victoria and Albert Museum
Arts Council of England
Museum of Modern Art, New York
Albright-Knox Gallery, Buffalo, New York
Contemporary Arts Society, London
The British Council
Fitzwilliam Museum, Cambridge
Arts Council of Northern Ireland
Walker Art Gallery, Liverpool
Felton Bequest, Melbourne, Australia
Arts Council Purchase Award (1965)
Nuffield Foundation
Nuffield Pictures for Hospitals for Children
Peter Stuyvesant Collection
Department of the Environment
Department of Education and Science
County Borough of Dudley
Carlisle Public Museums and Art Gallery
Leeds City Art Gallery
Leicester Museum and Art Gallery
Leicestershire Education Authority
Liverpool University
Graves Art Gallery, Sheffield
Chelsea and Westminster Hospital

EXHIBITIONS

GROUP SHOWS

1951 Institute of Contemporary Arts (ICA), London

1951 – 65 Regular Exhibitor with Gimpel Fils, London
Sandra Blow, Alan Davie and Redvers Taylor, Gimpel Fils, London
Blackhall, St Giles, Oxford
Adams, Blow, Paolozzi and Pasmore, Galleria Origine, Rome
Peter Kinley and Sandra Blow, Gimpel Fils, London
Summer Exhibition, Gimpel Fils, London

1957 The Art Foundation, Rome, *New Trends in British Art,* Rome – New York
The Art Club, Chicago, *Young British Painters* (toured U.S.A. for two years)
Young British Painters, toured Rotterdam, Zurich and Dusseldorf
XXIX Venice Biennale, Young Artists Section
John Moores Exhibition, Liverpool

1959 – 60 *Vitalita nell'Arte,* Palazzo Grassi, Venice; Kunsthalle, Recklinghausen
Stedeljk Museum, Amsterdam; Louisiana, Humblebaek, Denmark

1961 John Moores Exhibition (Second Prize Winner)
Carnegie Institute, Pittsburgh International

1962 Contemporary Art Society, Tate Gallery, *Painting in the '60s*
British Council Travelling Exhibition, Canada
Albright Knox Art Gallery, Buffalo, New York, *Contemporary British Painting*
North Carolina Museum of Art, Raleigh, North Carolina, *Young British Painters*
John Moores Exhibition, Liverpool (by invitation)

1967 *Aspects of New British Art,* British Council Touring Exhibition, Australia/New Zealand, Tate Gallery, Peter Stuyvesant Foundation Modern Collection, *Recent British Painting*

	Museum of Modern Art, Oxford, Prints Exhibition
	Camden Arts Centre, London, *English Landscape in the 20th Century*
	Institute of Directors Exhibition, Gulbenkian Hall, Royal College of Art
From 1971	Exhibits annually at The Summer Exhibition, Royal Academy
	Hayward Gallery, London, *British Painting '74*
	New Directions in Art, St Louis, Missouri
1977	Royal Academy of Art, London, *British Painting 1952 – 1977*
1978	Hayward Gallery, London, *The Hayward Annual, 1978*
1983	Royal Institute of Fine Arts, Glasgow
1985	Tate Gallery, London, *St Ives 1939 – 64, Twenty Five Years of Painting*
1988	Exhibition Road, Royal College of Art, London
	Fifteen British Artists, Gimpel Fils, London
	Birthright Exhibition, The Lefevre Gallery, London
1989	Albermale Gallery, London
1995	Tate St Ives, *Porthmeor Beach: A Century of Images*
	Illustrations for *Waves on Porthmeor Beach* Alaric Sumner (words worth books)
	BAA Commision: Glass Screen for Heathrow Airport
	Tate Gallery, London: Display of a painting on occasion of Sandra Blow's birthday
	Newlyn Art Gallery *Contours of Ideas from the Studio*
1996	Royal Academy Summer Show (including first etching)
	Exhibited in International Dubai Arts Centre, UAE
	Tate St Ives *Quality of Light* Display
1998	*Picture of the Year* Korn Ferry Award. Royal Academy Summer Exhibition
	British Council *British Painting in the Fifties* Exhibition, The Royal Hiberninan Academy, Dublin
	Ozten Zeki Gallery, London

	Kings College Portfolio, Gresham Studio, Cambridge
	Flowers East, London
1999	Adam Gallery, Bath
	City Gallery, London
	Royal Academy of Arts, London
2000	CCA Galleries, London
	Tate Britain: Display of a painting on the occasion of Sandra Blow's birthday
	Art Futures, Contemporary Art Society, London
	City Gallery, London
	Royal Academy of Arts, Summer Exhibition, London
	Fermyn Woods Contemporary Arts
2001	Highgate Fine Art, London
	Thomsons Gallery, London
	New Millennium Gallery, St Ives
	Lemon Street Gallery, Truro
	Tate St Ives collection display *Roger Mayne: St Ives Artists*

INDIVIDUAL SHOWS

1957	Saidenburg Gallery, New York
1960	International Guggenheim Award: Solomon R. Guggenheim Museum, New York, Gimpel Fils, London
	Individual Exhibition, Gimpel Fils, London
1966	New Art Centre, London
1968	Clare College, Cambridge
	New Art Centre, London
1971	New Art Centre, London
1973	New Art Centre, London
1979	Royal Academy, London, Diploma Gallery
1991	Francis Graham-Dixon Gallery, London
1994	*Sandra Blow: Retrospective*, The Sackler Galleries, Royal Academy, London
1997	New Millennium Gallery St Ives
2001	Tate St Ives *Sandra Blow: Space and Matter 1958–2001.* 15 December 2001 – 10 March 2002